# TROY AIKMAN

READ/San Diego
San Diego Public Library

# TROY AIKMAN

## QUICK-DRAW QUARTERBACK

Joel Dippold

Lerner Publications Company ■ Minneapolis

*To Valjoan Meyers*

*This book is available in two editions:*
Library binding by Lerner Publications Company
Soft cover by First Avenue Editions
241 First Avenue North
Minneapolis, Minnesota 55401

LIBRARY OF CONGRESS CATALOGING-IN-PUBLICATION DATA

**Dippold, Joel.**
   Troy Aikman, quick-draw quarterback / Joel Dippold.
      p. cm. — (The Achievers)
   ISBN 0-8225-2880-0 (library binding)
   ISBN 0-8225-9663-6 (paperback)
   1. Aikman, Troy, 1966- —Juvenile literature. 2. Football players—United States—Biography—Juvenile literature. 3. Dallas Cowboys (Football team)—Juvenile literature. [1. Aikman, Troy, 1966- . 2. Football players.] I. Title. II. Series.
GV939.A46D57 1994
796.332'92—dc20
[B]                                                                    93-47909

Manufactured in the United States of America
2  3  4  5  6  7  –  JR  –  01  00  99  98  97  96

# Contents

# 1

## Showdown in Pasadena

Quarterback Troy Aikman knew the whole world was watching him. It was Sunday, January 31, 1993, and he and the Dallas Cowboys were taking on the Buffalo Bills in the 1993 Super Bowl. The game, played at the Rose Bowl in Pasadena, California, would decide which football team was the best in the world.

More than 98,000 fans screamed and hollered from the bleachers, and millions of people across the country and around the world watched on television. On the field, Troy had to shout as loud as he could to be heard above the roar of the excited crowd.

Was Troy shaken up by all the pressure? "I almost passed out," he said after the game. "I tried to tell myself to just relax and play my game, but I was hyperventilating until the second quarter."

Troy had played in only one play-off game before this year—and in that game the Cowboys had been beaten badly. People said Troy's lack of play-off experience could cost Dallas the championship. And in the early stages of the game, the critics appeared to be right. Buffalo's defense smothered the Dallas offense. The Cowboys couldn't keep a drive going and had to punt the ball away twice.

"I was having a tough time getting into the feel of the ballgame," Troy said. The Buffalo linemen were all over him the instant the ball was snapped, and the Bills were double-teaming his wide receivers, Michael Irvin and Alvin Harper. When Troy did manage to throw the ball, half of his passes fell incomplete. With time running down in the first quarter, the Bills were leading Dallas 7-0.

The pressure was on, but performing under pressure is one of the things Troy Aikman does best. Charging 350-pound linemen don't seem to faze him. He takes the hardest hits without flinching. Even in his rookie year, he had played with the cool head and determination of a veteran.

Still, nothing could prepare him for the emotional impact of playing in the Super Bowl—the realization of his lifelong goal. "It was almost like a dream," Troy said. "They announced my name and I ran out onto the field at the Rose Bowl, and there was a tremendous rush, unlike anything I've ever known....It took me about a quarter and a half before I really came back to earth."

Finally, the significance of the event hit home. Here was Troy's chance to make his football dreams come true—or have them turn into nightmares. Would the sheer excitement of playing in the Super Bowl rattle Troy Aikman in a way charging linemen could not?

The challenges of quarterbacking are often more mental than physical.

Near the end of the first quarter, Troy finally started to move his team. He began to pick apart the Buffalo defense with quick passes to tight end Jay Novacek and handoffs to running back Emmitt Smith. He drove his team half the length of the field, then drilled a perfectly timed 23-yard pass to Novacek. Touchdown, Cowboys!

The Cowboys' defense scored the next touchdown only 15 seconds later, after forcing a Buffalo fumble. Buffalo kicked a field goal early in the second quarter, then Troy took his turn again. He marched his team 72 yards in only five plays. From 19 yards out, he passed to Michael Irvin for another touchdown. The score was 21-10, Dallas.

Only 18 seconds later, the Cowboys got the ball back on a turnover, and Troy rifled a long pass to Irvin in the end zone. Another touchdown!

"When I really get on a roll throwing the football, I feel I can take control of the game and that I'm going to complete every pass I throw," Troy said. "And in the second quarter, that's when I got into that groove and I felt there was no way they were going to be able to stop us offensively. And they didn't."

Troy had completed 14 of 19 throws and had scored three touchdowns in the half. Far from collapsing under pressure, he had met the challenge and sent the Buffalo Bills reeling instead.

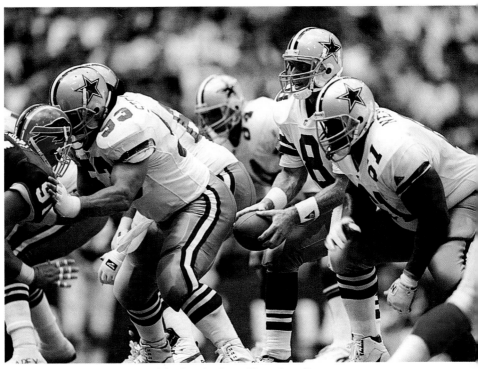
Troy works behind a hefty offensive line.

In the second half, the Cowboys continued to dominate. Troy completed 8 of 11 passes and scored another touchdown on a 45-yard bomb to Alvin Harper.

The final score was Dallas 52, Buffalo 17—one of the biggest romps in Super Bowl history. The Cowboys were the world champions. Troy Aikman, named the game's Most Valuable Player, had become a football superstar.

The top quarterback in the NFL doesn't get much peace and quiet after a game.

What made Troy's victory in the Super Bowl unlike any other in National Football League history? After all, one quarterback or another wins the Super Bowl every year. What made Troy's accomplishments so special?

For one thing, at age 26, he was the youngest Super Bowl MVP since the great Joe Montana won the honor in 1982 at age 25. By the end of the game, Troy had also set an NFL record of 89 postseason passes without an interception, breaking Montana's record of 83.

Troy's performance leading up to the Super Bowl was just as impressive. In the Cowboys' three playoff games, going up against the toughest football teams in the league, Troy had completed 68 percent of his passes for 795 yards, eight touchdowns, and no interceptions. His overall performance made him the highest rated postseason quarterback in the history of the NFL.

After the Super Bowl, Troy reflected on how he felt about his promotion to the ranks of football's most brilliant quarterbacks. "I've always believed I could play with the best quarterbacks in the league," he said. "But it was strange being out there on the field while guys I grew up watching, John Elway and Dan Marino, were watching me."

If Troy thought the Super Bowl excitement would die down once the final whistle had blown on Sunday, he was wrong. He soon began to see that being a football hero took almost as much effort as becoming one.

Even before he had time to shower, Troy was rushed to a press conference, where he tried to explain how it felt to be named the Super Bowl MVP. Wearing a baseball hat to cover his dirty hair, Troy told the reporters, "This game meant everything to me. It's a tremendous weight off my shoulders. No matter what happens for the rest of my career, at least I can say I took my team to a Super Bowl, and I was able to win." A second later, he added, "But now that I've won one—I don't want to be greedy, but I'd like to win two."

After the press conference, he went back to his hotel room for a private victory celebration with a few close friends. Did he order lobster tails and champagne? Not Troy—just hamburgers and beer from room service.

Is Joe Montana the greatest NFL quarterback of all time? Not for long.

Next he was off to the Cowboys' victory party to celebrate the win with his teammates. But his arrival caused such a frenzy among fans and the press that he had to leave after a few minutes.

He went back to his hotel room and tried to sleep. But he was too excited. At 2:00 A.M., he had to get dressed again—to get ready for appearances on three early-morning TV news programs.

By mid-morning on Monday, Troy was thoroughly exhausted and disoriented. Troy's business agent, Leigh Steinberg, remembers one interviewer telling Troy he'd watched the game the night before, and Troy replied, "Wait a second, is it tomorrow already?"

After staggering back to his room, Troy managed to get an hour and a half of sleep. But soon it was 11:00 and time for more interviews—five hours of interviews. "I'd pick up the phone, do the interview, put it down, and it would ring again. I was all by myself in my room. I didn't know where to go. I didn't have a car, and there were people lingering in the hotel, wanting autographs. I felt trapped."

By now, Troy was thinking that a few 350-pound linebackers were nothing compared to this media blitz. All the attention made Troy uncomfortable. After all, in his own mind, he was just another country boy from Oklahoma.

By his junior year in high school, Troy had offers from many college football teams.

# *Young Gun*

Troy Kenneth Aikman was born on November 21, 1966, in Cerritos, California, a suburb of Los Angeles. He is the youngest of Kenneth and Charlyn Aikman's three children; he has two older sisters.

Troy was born with a condition—similar to clubfoot—that caused his feet to grow crooked. To correct the problem, doctors put Troy into casts up to his knees when he was eight months old. When he started learning to walk, soon after his first birthday, the casts were replaced by special shoes—shoes that looked like they were on the wrong feet. At night when Troy went to sleep, his mother would strap the heels of the shoes together to help his feet grow straight.

Fortunately for Troy—and for the Dallas Cowboys and their fans—the special shoes worked.

Troy soon walked and ran around just like any other child. He loved to play sports, especially football. By the time Troy was nine years old, he dreamed of being a professional football player. "I used to practice my signature, working on the way I wanted to sign my autograph," Troy remembers. "I'd say to myself, 'One day I'll be somebody. They'll want my autograph.'"

Troy's father was a welder. He worked in pipeline construction, laying gas and sewer pipe. When Troy was 12 and about to enter eighth grade, his father took a new job. The Aikmans left bustling southern California for rural Oklahoma. They moved into a house on a 172-acre ranch outside of the small town of Henryetta, about 100 miles north of Dallas, Texas. There, the Aikmans raised cattle, pigs, and chickens.

The change came as a shock to young Troy. He missed his friends, and he also missed the excitement of living near a big city like Los Angeles. Oklahoma seemed boring. "We had no neighbors," Troy recalls. "I didn't like Oklahoma at all."

Although Henryetta's social life was dull sometimes, Troy soon found some activities to fill his time. When he wasn't in school or doing chores on the family's ranch, he collected baseball cards. In high school, Troy lettered in three sports: baseball, basketball, and, of course, football.

Troy soon grew to like the quiet life of Oklahoma.

People from Texas and Oklahoma are famous for being crazy about football, and Troy was no exception. His goal was to play someday for his favorite team, the Dallas Cowboys.

At Henryetta High, Troy quarterbacked a team named the Fighting Hens. In spite of Troy's talents, the Hens didn't win many games. Their coach, Bill Holt, remembers one of Troy's earliest games: "Against Hartshorne, we were seven points down in the last two minutes of the game. We were throwing the ball. Two of Hartshorne's guys had him and were taking him down. As Troy was falling…he threw a 25-yard sidearm touchdown pass. I live near Hartshorne now. Those kids still talk about that play. We still lost by a point, but after the game, their coach told Troy, 'We'll be watching you someday on *Monday Night Football*.'" The coach from Hartshorne turned out to be right!

Troy was a very talented baseball player, too. He played pitcher and shortstop. Coach Rick Enis remembers college baseball scouts coming to see Troy play when he was only a sophomore. Troy could have gone to college on a baseball scholarship if he hadn't been determined to make his name as a quarterback. "Football was just his first love," Enis remembers.

Enis recalls another of Troy's talents. "He took a typing class with 38 girls, and I remember they went to a contest at Okmulgee State Tech, about 15 miles from here. They came back, and at a lunch assembly, they announced the third-place winner, some little girl. Then second place was a little girl, and then the winner was—Troy. I kind of dropped my fork, although it was kind of embarrassing for him. [I still have] a picture of him from that day."

When Troy moved to Oklahoma, the legendary Roger Staubach was winding down his career as a quarterback with the Dallas Cowboys. Staubach's name is all over the Cowboy record books. He led the Cowboys to the play-offs every season from 1971 to 1979 and won two Super Bowls. Dallas fans gave him the nickname "Captain Comeback," because he often led his team to dramatic, come-from-behind victories in the final minutes of the game. Many people consider Roger Staubach to be the greatest Cowboy quarterback of all time—for now.

Troy knew that Roger Staubach had worked hard to become a great football player, and he would have to work hard, too. Enis, who coached football and baseball at Henryetta, described Troy's determination: "When we would get through with practice, Troy would say, 'Coach, could you keep your receivers out so we can throw?' every day after practice in 100-degree weather."

Roger Staubach led the Dallas Cowboys to great victories.

Troy was also influenced by the example of the strongest, toughest man he knew: his father. "Part of the reason I play the way that I play and don't fear getting [tackled]—people say I take unnecessary hits—I think that stems from back when I was younger and seeing how hard he worked and how tough he was and wanting to prove to him that I was tough too," Troy says.

"I think that deep down, I always wanted to prove that I was as tough as he was....And I think that through football I was able to prove that to him."

Troy was a quiet, polite teenager. "He was *very* quiet. You never knew he was around," recalls Rick Enis. Troy's athletic ability made him a leader of whatever team he joined. "But he had a lot of difficulty accepting his role," Enis says. "If he had been more vocal he would have been an even better leader."

But Troy's soft-spoken manner suited tiny Henryetta. Although he had been bored at first, Troy soon came to love Oklahoma. "I identified with the people so well, that type of lifestyle," he says. "The laid-back, easygoing people. The values they share in small towns. I enjoyed everything about growing up in a small town in rural America."

But Troy's athletic ability was about to carry him out of small-town America—and into the big time.

# 3

# *Air Aikman*

While he was still a sophomore at Henryetta High, Troy met the head football coach at Oklahoma State University, a man named Jimmy Johnson. Johnson was an energetic man who lived and breathed football. He had a reputation for bringing out the best in people—by stressing their positive traits instead of their negatives. And above all, he had a fierce desire to win.

Would Troy be interested in playing football for Johnson's team? Troy said that he would—but he didn't put his promise in writing. Later, he changed his mind and accepted a scholarship to the University of Oklahoma, which had one of the best football teams in the nation.

Troy turned down
OSU's coach Jimmy
Johnson to play
across state with the
Oklahoma Sooners.

The head coach at Oklahoma, Barry Switzer, used a running attack called the wishbone offense. Switzer told Troy that with his strong arm at quarterback, Oklahoma would abandon the wishbone and go to an offense that emphasized passing.

But once he joined the team, in the fall of 1984, Troy found himself running the wishbone offense after all. "He lied to me, no question about that, when he recruited me," Troy says of Switzer. "He tells me he's going to a passing game, and four days into workouts, he's back to the wishbone. But I will say this for the man, he was very upfront about everything after that. I liked him, actually. Still do."

Things began badly for Troy at Oklahoma, and they didn't get much better. He started in only one game during his freshman season, and Oklahoma took a beating in that game. He spent most of the season on the bench, watching his more experienced teammates play.

But Coach Switzer and others had high hopes for Troy. At 6 feet, 3 inches, and weighing more than 200 pounds, he was built like a running back. Troy's size would be a big asset in the wishbone offense, the coach thought, since the quarterback must often run with the ball. And Troy's arm strength and accurate passing had earned him the nickname "Air Aikman."

The Oklahoma Sooners were the top-rated college team in the nation at the start of the 1985 season, mostly because of their strong defense. And Troy was the team's starting quarterback.

The Sooners won the season opener against Minnesota. But the score was close—too close. They lost their number one ranking, and rumors started going around that Troy's job at quarterback was up for grabs. Troy's critics said he was too slow on his feet to run the wishbone and not consistent in his passing.

Troy's performance at Oklahoma didn't quite live up to the coaches' expectations.

The Sooners won their next two games but faced their toughest challenge in the fourth game of the season. They went up against a great team from the University of Miami, coached by the same Jimmy Johnson who had almost lured Troy to Oklahoma State. Troy knew that to win he would have to score a lot of points for the Sooners, because Miami's brilliant offense was sure to score plenty of its own.

Troy got off to a great start in the game. He completed every one of his first six passes for 131 yards and one touchdown. His seventh pass was almost in the hands of a receiver in the end zone, but a Miami player made a spectacular flying leap and knocked the ball down with his fingertips.

But on the next play, Troy was sacked by two Miami defenders. He hit the ground hard and doubled up, clutching his left leg in agony. The leg was broken. Troy's football season was suddenly over. And without Troy to direct the offense, the Sooners lost the game to Miami, 27-14.

While his broken leg healed, Troy had some time to think. Should he stay at Oklahoma and stick with the frustrating wishbone offense? At the end of the season, he announced his decision. Even though he'd be redshirted—in other words, he'd have to sit out a year—he would transfer to another school.

Troy decided to attend the University of California at Los Angeles (UCLA), but not before Jimmy Johnson again asked Troy to play for him—this time at Miami. Troy turned Johnson down. "I didn't like the city," Troy says. "The environment, the atmosphere—those kinds of things mean a lot to me." At UCLA, where he would study sociology, Troy would be playing near his childhood home.

Los Angeles might have been familiar to Troy, but nothing else about UCLA was. In many ways, transferring to Los Angeles meant starting all over as a rookie. At Oklahoma, Troy had played in only five games. But he had become familiar with the playbook, the list of plays his team used. Now he had a whole new playbook to memorize. He also had to learn the strengths and weaknesses of each teammate and get to know the opposing teams in a new football conference.

But Troy was comfortable with UCLA's style of offense, and he didn't worry about Coach Terry Donahue taking the starting job away from him. "He and I were very close," Troy says of Coach Donahue. "He has proven to me, time and time again, that he cares about Troy Aikman, the person rather than the quarterback."

Troy's two seasons at UCLA were very productive. He had been a quarterback with promise at Oklahoma, but he fulfilled that promise at UCLA.

He set school records for touchdown passes in a season, completed passes in a season, and completed passes in a single game. In fact, when he graduated in 1989, he ranked either first or second in 12 different categories in the UCLA record books.

When Troy reached UCLA he hit his stride.

In only two seasons, he came close to breaking records for touchdown passes and yards passing that had been set by quarterbacks who played at UCLA for four years. With Troy at quarterback, the UCLA Bruins had 20 victories and just four losses and went on to win bowl games at the end of both seasons.

In his senior year, Troy was awarded the Davey O'Brien National Quarterback Award, given to the best college quarterback in the country. He was also named College Quarterback of the Year by the Quarterback Club of Washington, D.C. And he finished third in voting for the Heisman Trophy, given to the best college player in any position.

The last two games of his senior season were the most important to Troy. In the final regular season game, UCLA was matched against its cross-town rival, the University of Southern California (USC). Games between the two teams were always bitterly fought contests. This year, both sides were looking for a showdown. People said Troy was the country's best college quarterback, but USC had one of the nation's top-ranked defenses.

The pressure had never been greater, and Troy responded by playing the best game of his college career. He completed 32 passes, breaking a school record. He passed for 317 yards and scored two touchdowns. But Troy's passing alone could not carry the team. The Bruins only gained 73 yards running and lost by a score of 31-22. Troy hadn't won the game. But his personal performance had proven that he was a winner all the same.

The Bruins had still played well enough throughout the season to earn an invitation to the Cotton Bowl. Their opponent was a tough Arkansas team. In that game, Troy completed 19 of 27 passes—an incredible 70 percent completion rate. The Bruins walked away with the victory by beating Arkansas 17-3, and Troy was voted the game's Most Valuable Offensive Player.

Just as important as the win was the fact that the game was played before a cheering crowd in Dallas, Texas. Many of Troy's friends from Henryetta had driven down to see him wrap up his college career. And a lot of Dallas fans got their first look at the future Cowboy superstar.

"The Cowboys will win big," Jerry Jones promises the news media.

# Texas Blues

In 1989 the Dallas Cowboys needed help. The Cowboys had been the most powerful team in football throughout the 1970s. But by the mid-1980s, the franchise had fallen on hard times. In 1986 Dallas had its first losing season in more than 20 years. In 1988 the team won only three games. Cowboy fans were used to seeing their team win. They started to grumble, and they stopped coming to see the team play.

At the end of the 1988 season, an Arkansas oil millionaire named Jerry Jones bought the Dallas Cowboys. Jones did things with style, and he wasn't afraid to take risks. In the final negotiations for the sale of the team, the previous owner wanted $500,000 more than Jones had offered to pay. So the two men agreed to flip a coin to decide on the price. Jones lost the flip and paid $140 million for the Cowboys!

Jerry Jones knew his new franchise was in serious trouble and that something had to change. But what? Jones's answer was: everything. He started by firing Tom Landry, head coach of the Cowboys since their first season in 1960. Dallas fans were outraged. No one thought Landry deserved to be fired. After all, he had made the Cowboys into more than just another NFL football team. The Cowboys had once been so good that people called them "America's Team."

Jones had his own ideas, though. He replaced Landry with an old friend from his days playing football for the University of Arkansas. That friend's name was Jimmy Johnson, former head coach at Oklahoma State and Miami.

Jones and Johnson knew they needed some new talent on their team, and they wanted the very best. Only two weeks after Johnson signed his own contract with the Cowboys, he welcomed his first new player to the team. The Cowboys used the very first pick in the 1989 draft to sign a rookie quarterback—Troy Aikman.

The Cowboys offered Troy a six-year, $11.2-million contract with a bonus payment of almost $3 million. No rookie had ever been offered so much money, and six years was an unusually long-term deal. But Jones and Johnson wanted Troy in a Cowboys uniform—no matter what it took.

Jerry Rhome, the Cowboys' quarterback coach, described Troy this way: "If you sat down to build an NFL quarterback, Troy is what you'd come up with. He's six feet, four inches, 222 pounds, great arm strength—everything's perfect."

With his youth and talent, Troy represented the future of the team. "Troy Aikman helps restore the Cowboy image," said Jerry Jones at the contract-signing ceremony. "He's got this winning aura."

"We never really had any question about Troy being our first pick," Coach Johnson added. Then he described how he had asked Troy to play for him at Oklahoma State and again at Miami. "I was afraid he would turn me down a third time," Johnson said.

Perhaps Troy was destined to play for Jimmy Johnson. But Johnson or not, Troy had never wanted to play professionally anywhere but Dallas. He described becoming the Cowboys' quarterback as "a dream come true."

Then, referring to the game against Miami that ended his frustrating Oklahoma career, he told Johnson, "Thanks for breaking my leg, Coach. You did me a favor."

Even the departing Tom Landry couldn't help but admire the Cowboys' new prospect. He even referred to Troy as "the next Roger Staubach." Such high praise made Troy uncomfortable—but also proud. "I don't like comparisons," he said, "but I love being mentioned in the same breath as Roger Staubach."

Troy's career had been on an upswing ever since he transferred to UCLA. But hard times were just around the corner. A few months after the Cowboys signed Troy, they drafted Steve Walsh, the quarterback from Jimmy Johnson's Miami team.

Walsh was also very talented. He had won 23 of 24 games in his two years under Johnson. He had led Miami to a national championship in 1987. While he was slower than Troy and couldn't throw the ball as far, people said he had a better mind for the game and greater accuracy. Which quarterback would become the team's leader and which would be the second-string player? Coach Johnson wasn't giving any clues. "They know they'll get an equal chance," he told reporters.

By the end of the preseason, Troy had won the starting quarterback job. But Walsh was always in the background, ready to step in if Troy showed any sign of weakness.

"I thought Jimmy had a natural allegiance to Steve," Troy said, "but the fact that he didn't make that clear, or who he wanted for the future, made the situation very tense. I was not close to Jimmy at all that first year and I was not happy. Something had to give."

Troy was very frustrated during his rookie season with Dallas.

Troy's unhappiness was far from over. Every Sunday, opposing linemen would pound him mercilessly. Like the rest of the team, the Cowboys' offensive linemen were young and inexperienced. They couldn't protect their quarterback when he dropped back to pass. Troy stood in the pocket waiting for his receivers to get open, and he took a lot of hard hits in the process.

"There was a Philadelphia game, the first time we played them, on Thanksgiving. I walked into the locker room after the game and they X-rayed both shoulders, both knees, my elbow. I thought they were going to put me in a body cast." Troy was taking a beating. But he was taking it—he wasn't giving up.

Yet as the Cowboys continued to lose game after game, Troy's frustration sometimes boiled over. The temptation to quit was always there. But when Leigh Steinberg asked him, "Troy, do you want a trade? What do you want me to do about this?" Troy backed down. He said he wanted to keep playing for the Cowboys.

Meanwhile, the Cowboys continued to lose football games. On his way to a fourth loss in four games, Troy broke the index finger of his left hand. Since Troy is right-handed, it was a lucky break. Even so, he had to sit on the sidelines for the next five games and watch Steve Walsh lead the team. Walsh quarterbacked the Cowboys to their first win of the year by beating the Washington Redskins.

The next week, Troy was healthy enough to play again. He was eager for action and came out throwing against the Phoenix Cardinals. He passed for 379 yards that day, setting an NFL record for passing yards gained by a rookie.

With less than two minutes left in the game, Dallas was trailing 17-13. Troy wanted this game, though. He wasn't going to let anyone take it from him.

What happened next may rank as the most spectacular play of Troy's career. Over the heads of a pair of charging linebackers, Troy saw a receiver open far downfield. He launched the ball a split second before he was hit—and hit hard. The pass was complete for 80 yards and a touchdown. The Cowboys took a 20-17 lead. But Troy never saw the completion. He had been knocked unconscious by the blow and lay senseless on the field.

"There were a lot of people scared," Troy remembers. "They thought I was either dead or paralyzed. I just didn't move for 10 minutes. When I finally came around, Coach Johnson was leaning over me and he said, 'Nice pass.'" Troy was helped from the field with blood running out of his ear.

Then, with only seconds left in the game, Troy

watched from the sidelines as Phoenix scored a touchdown of its own on another long pass. Phoenix won the game, 24-20. Troy was crushed.

"That was probably as low as I got," he says. "I knew it couldn't get any worse. If I'd had to go through another year like that, I would have played out my contract and been done with football forever. I was so badly beaten up that I couldn't understand how some of my teammates had lasted 10 years in the NFL. I knew I'd never make it that long."

In Tom Landry's last year as coach, Dallas had posted a win-loss record of 3-13. But in the team's first year under Jimmy Johnson, its record was only 1-15. The victory over Washington had been Dallas's one and only win of the season.

"I couldn't imagine the Dallas Cowboys ever being as bad as we've been," Troy said near the end of the season. But Troy showed he had kept his sense of humor by telling this joke: "Did you hear Jerry Jones bought a Seven-Eleven and turned it into a Zero-and-Eleven?"

Troy saw past his frustrations and recognized that, no matter how painful, the disastrous season had also made him stronger. "I grew up a lot last year," he said. "In the long run, it has made me a better player to go through the year I went through."

Emmitt Smith—the superweapon of the Dallas running attack

Fortunately, things started to turn around for Troy and his teammates in 1990. The Cowboys drafted running back Emmitt Smith, giving the offense a rushing threat to complement Troy's passing talents. And just a few days before the first game of the season, Steve Walsh was traded to the New Orleans Saints. Now Troy was the undisputed team leader.

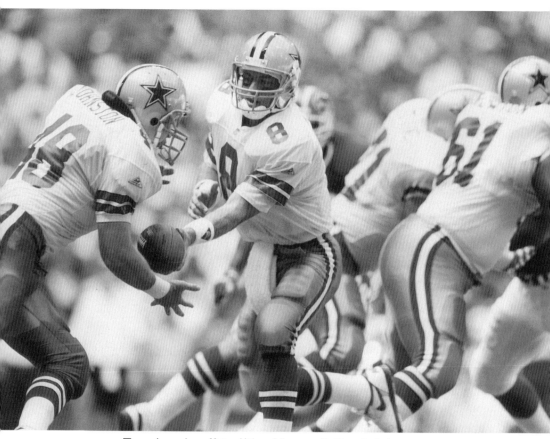

Troy hands off to "the Moose," Daryl Johnston.

In 1990 the Cowboys won seven games. In six of those games, Troy brought the team from behind in the fourth quarter. He was beginning to look like another Captain Comeback! He was starting to show the qualities he would become famous for: calmness, courage, and consistency.

# 5

## *Tall in the Saddle*

The 1991 season saw more changes for Troy and the Cowboys. The most important change for Troy was the hiring of Norv Turner as offensive coordinator. Turner designed a new offensive strategy for the Cowboys to make the best use of Troy's talents. The new game plan emphasized short passes and precision timing.

Long passes give the receiver time to react if the quarterback throws off target or doesn't get the pass off in time. Short passes put more responsibility on the quarterback. For Turner's strategy to work, Troy would have to throw right on target, right on time. And he did. In his first year playing under the new system, Troy had the most passing yards and highest completion rate of any quarterback in the National Football Conference (NFC).

Jimmy Johnson (left), Norv Turner

The new system also helped protect Troy from injury. When a pass is thrown quickly, defensive linemen have less time to push past blockers and get to the quarterback. So Troy received fewer lumps and bruises than he did during his first two years as a pro.

In the 1991 season, the Cowboys and Troy started to show their Super Bowl form. They beat the defending champions, the New York Giants, 21-16. In that game, Troy passed for 277 yards and completed 74 percent of his attempts. With the Cowboys trailing the Giants late in the fourth quarter, Troy led his team on an 84-yard drive, connecting on five out of six passes. He capped the drive with a touchdown toss to Michael Irvin to put the game away.

In Dallas's next contest, against Green Bay, Troy was successful on over 75 percent of his passes. He completed 31, the most in his career for one game. At the end of the game, he completed 12 straight passes, and the Cowboys won by a close score.

The next week, Troy led a fourth-quarter come-back to win a big game against the Cincinnati Bengals. In the process, he tallied a career-high 12.6 yards per completion.

But Troy's regular season ended early, when he sprained his right knee in late November. Backup quarterback Steve Beuerlein took over for the last four games of the season. The Cowboys won all four and made the play-offs for the first time in six years. Troy was well enough to play by the second play-off game, against the Detroit Lions. But the Cowboys lost by a lopsided score of 38-6.

Troy finished the season with a completion percentage of 65.3, the best in Cowboy history. He had started the season by throwing 93 passes without an interception and later had a streak of 116. His performance that year earned him his first trip to the Pro Bowl.

The Cowboys had racked up a win-loss record of 11-5 for the season. But many people thought their success was just a fluke. Rebuilding a professional football team usually takes many years. The Cowboys had been 1-15 only two years before. Critics said the team was still too young. They said the Cowboys still had many weaknesses and that they shouldn't expect to do as well in 1992.

Troy and his teammates began to prove the critics wrong in the very first game of the 1992 season. In front of a national TV audience, on *Monday Night Football,* Dallas beat the defending Super Bowl champions, the Washington Redskins, 23-10. Troy went on to lead his team to victories in seven of the next eight games. The Cowboys were riding high!

Troy only got better as the season went on. He beat Denver by leading the Cowboys on a long drive at the end of the game. Then he completed an amazing 85 percent of his passes—including 13 in a row—to defeat Atlanta.

Next came the play-offs. The Cowboys walked over the Philadelphia Eagles, 34-10, to win the NFC Eastern Division. Troy led the march on four long scoring drives in that game. "For me, it was the biggest win I ever experienced," he said afterward. Even bigger wins were just ahead.

The Cowboys were on their way to the top. "I think we are close to being America's Team again," said owner Jerry Jones.

Emmitt Smith blocks while Troy fires the ball.

The NFC championship game was a showdown with San Francisco. The 49ers had been the dominant team throughout the 1980s. They had won the Super Bowl four times, and their quarterback, Steve Young, was rated the number one passer in the league. Longtime Dallas fans were especially nervous. The Cowboys had lost to the 49ers 12 years in a row. Would this year be any different?

The two teams battled it out in the first half, and at halftime the score was tied at 10-10. But then Troy got into a groove. In the second half, he threw 16 passes and completed 13. With San Francisco threatening a comeback late in the fourth quarter, Troy saw a hole in the 49er pass protection and made the defense pay with a 70-yard bomb to Alvin Harper. A few seconds later, he threw a touchdown pass to put the game away. The final score was Dallas 30, San Francisco 20. The Dallas Cowboys were going to the Super Bowl!

Troy had completed a play-off record 70 percent of his passes and had thrown for a whopping 322 yards. "If anyone questioned the coolness and maturity of Troy Aikman, they better look at that third period again," said Troy's teammate Mark Tuinei. "He never flinched. Every time we needed a big play on third down, he got it for us."

"Simply incredible," was how Norv Turner described Troy's efforts. "I can't imagine a quarterback playing better than Troy played, especially down the stretch."

In fact, Troy's performance in the play-offs was the best in the history of the NFL. He set play-off records for the most yards per pass thrown, the highest percentage of passes caught, the lowest interception rate, and the highest overall quarterback rating.

"Troy has come a long way, and he has brought me with him," Coach Johnson said. "[He's] the best quarterback I've ever coached and the best quarterback in the league."

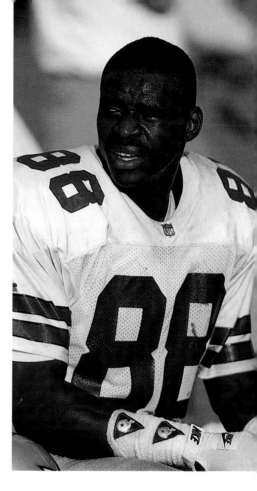

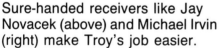
Sure-handed receivers like Jay Novacek (above) and Michael Irvin (right) make Troy's job easier.

The worst mistake a quarterback can make is to throw an interception. Many games have been lost by a poorly thrown pass. But Troy almost never throws an interception. He ended the 1992 season by safely throwing 137 passes in a row.

"Troy's the most accurate thrower in football," New York Giants quarterback Phil Simms says. "When you put strength and accuracy together, Troy's the best in the game. I marvel at him."

49

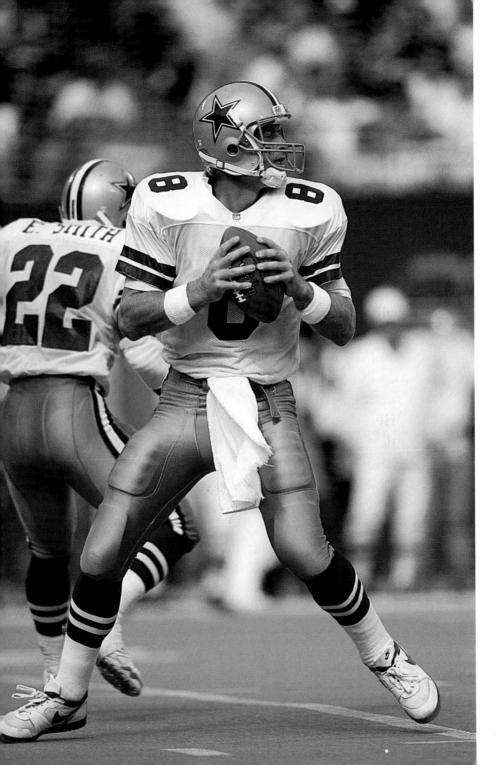

Troy is also one of the NFL's most well-rounded quarterbacks. He can "read" the defense (predict what the defenders are going to do by the way they line up before the snap); he can throw both long and short passes with accuracy; and he can instantly find the open receiver in a crowd of defenders. He has become the standard against which other coaches judge their quarterbacks. Leigh Steinberg explains: "People around the league are talking about an 'Aikman type': big and strong, physically gifted, can throw long and short, doesn't fold under pressure."

But all the physical ability in the world wouldn't do Troy any good if he didn't have mental toughness. His faith in himself is as strong as his throwing arm. "He's never had an ounce of doubt in his body about his own ability," says Norv Turner. "You wouldn't make the throws he makes unless you had unbelievable confidence."

After the 1993 Super Bowl, no one would ever again say that Troy Aikman wasn't ready for the big time. He *was* the big time!

# Ride 'Em Cowboy

There's an old saying: Be careful what you wish for, because you just might get it. Troy had dreamed of being famous. But he soon learned that being famous wasn't easy. For days after the 1993 Super Bowl, Troy raced from interview to interview. His schedule was already filled for the next several months. When would he be able to kick back, relax, and enjoy the victory?

There was no break in sight. Hundreds of requests flooded into Troy's business office. Nike and Reebok competed to sign him to an endorsement contract. So did Coke and Pepsi. Nintendo marketed a video football game with Troy's name on it. The people of Troy, Texas, even voted to change the name of their town to Troy Aikman, Texas, for the length of the football season.

Leigh Steinberg described Troy as "a marketing dream" and predicted that he would earn at least a million dollars a year from endorsements, public appearances, and other business deals. Troy appeared on Oprah Winfrey's show to talk about fantasy romance, and the tabloid press gossiped about which famous actresses and singers he might be dating. "Hollywood could have created him," one reporter said. "A blond, blue-eyed cowboy with perfect teeth and a hot hand, Troy looks exactly like the hero he's become."

But Hollywood didn't create Troy Aikman, Henryetta did. When another reporter asked Troy if he'd get a ticker-tape parade back in Henryetta after the Super Bowl, Troy answered with a grin: "Doubt it. Henryetta will be the same as it's always been."

And Troy wants to stay the same, too. "You see a lot of the top quarterbacks today...and you get the feeling that their minds aren't completely into it," remarks former Cowboy Cliff Harris. "It's this deal and that deal and the endorsement packages they've got lined up. Troy's not like that."

"I don't think I'll lose sight of what got me here," Troy explains. "I'll stay in Dallas in the off-season, maybe drop back to Oklahoma once in a while to see my friends." Indeed, despite fame and riches, Troy is just as humble and soft-spoken as ever. Many athletes brag and use vulgar language, but Troy doesn't swear. He says things like "Oh, shoot, now," when he gets flustered. And when Troy heard that *People* magazine had named him one of the "50 Most Beautiful People of 1993," his modest response was: "Well, they don't know that many people."

Troy lives in Dallas these days, in a house decorated in Western style. He has many interests outside of football. He enjoyed the musical "The Phantom of the Opera" and read Vice President Al Gore's book, *Earth in the Balance*. Leigh Steinberg says Troy "is very much into computers," including a laptop model he uses to keep track of his personal appointments and workouts. (He's still a typing whiz and can type 80 words a minute.)

Some days Troy drives around town in a white BMW. But most of the time he's behind the wheel of a beefy pickup truck. He owns a pair of lizard-skin boots for every day of the week, and he's a country music fanatic.

Right after the Super Bowl, Troy and Leigh Steinberg left the stadium in the back of a limousine. Steinberg was trying to tell Troy about the business opportunities open to him as a Super Bowl champ. But Troy was busy looking for a country station on the radio.

"Periodically, the discussion would be interrupted with Troy saying, 'Wait a second, I like this song,'" recalls Steinberg. "Or I'd be [saying], 'You have a $2 million endorsement,' and he's [saying], 'Wait a second, it's time for Garth [Brooks].'"

Troy likes to sing country songs as well as listen to them. With the help of some professional musicians, he and tight end Jay Novacek, special teams coach Joe Avezzano, and former Cowboys Walt Garrison and Randy White recorded a country and western album. They called themselves the Super Boys, and their album is titled, *Everybody Wants to Be a Cowboy*. Troy sings a ballad called "Oklahoma Nights" on the record.

How does his singing compare to his quarterbacking? "I've fallen under some criticism," he says, smiling. "That's okay. When they're critical of how I play quarterback, I'm concerned. When they're critical of how I sing, that doesn't bother me a bit."

In many ways, this Dallas Cowboy acts like an actual cowboy. But Troy is quick to correct this image. "Sometimes they paint me to be a true-to-life cowboy," he says. "I can't even ride a horse."

When he's not singing or playing football, Troy works with charities such as the American Cancer Society, Easter Seals, Special Olympics, and the United Way, just to name a few. He has set up an athletic scholarship fund at UCLA and an academic scholarship at Henryetta High for college-bound seniors. He also pledged $20,000 to build a health and fitness center for young people in Henryetta. Troy's work has twice made him a finalist for the NFL's Man of the Year award, which honors players for contributing to their communities.

Most days, there are no gaps in Troy's packed schedule. When he does get some free time, he can't go out in public without drawing a crowd. If he goes out to eat in a restaurant, his food often grows cold while he signs autographs. All that practice when he was nine years old is coming in handy now!

Troy signs a Super Boys cassette for a fan.

The Super Boys—Randy White, Joe Avezzano, Troy, Jay Novacek, and Walt Garrison—are proud of their singing talents.

Troy makes every effort to oblige his fans. When he doesn't have time to talk, he might get the fan's name and address. Then he'll send an autographed action picture of himself when he gets back to his office. Troy's good looks and bachelor status make him especially popular with female fans. Some women even wave signs at Cowboy games that say, "Marry me, Troy!"

Troy tries to limit the amount of attention he attracts—and not just for his own sake. "I've been real aware of the public," he explains. "If I were a nine-to-five working individual, I'd get tired of seeing me on TV all the time....I hope to be in Dallas for a long time, and I don't want to wear out my welcome.

"There is a fun side to doing all the commercials, getting the interview requests, and playing up the glamour boy thing," he admits. "But it is a battle that goes on inside of me. I want the successful off-field part. But I've also seen what happens when a guy gets taken over by those distractions. So nothing is going to change my real goal, which is to get back to and win another Super Bowl."

One of the few things that could stop him would be an injury. During the 1992 season, Troy stayed healthy all year and the Cowboys won the championship. But before the 1993 season had even started, he badly injured his back lifting 300 pounds in the Cowboys' weight room.

Troy checked into the hospital and then flew to Los Angeles for an operation called a lumbar diskectomy. Using a microscope, a surgeon removed a piece of gristle the size of an almond from Troy's spinal column.

The doctors told Troy to stay away from football for 12 weeks. But Troy wanted to be ready for the 1993 season. After just eight weeks, he asked to be put into a preseason game against the Houston

Oilers, the Cowboys' cross-state rivals. The doctors were cautious, but Troy said, "I'm ready to roll."

Before the game, Coach Johnson warned Troy not to take any risks with his weak back. But with the Cowboys behind in the second quarter, Troy saw a chance to pick up a first down by running the ball himself. One Houston player brought Troy down hard, and another hit him in the back as he fell. The stadium was quiet. The fans waited to see if Troy was all right. Fortunately, he was—and he even got the first down. Then, on the very next play, Troy took off running again, and took another hard hit from a Houston tackler!

Most people thought Troy made a bad decision to risk an injury in the preseason, when the games don't count. But Troy thinks that being a winner means taking chances once in a while—and playing hard all the time.

The regular season started badly for the Cowboys. Emmitt Smith sat out because of a contract dispute, and Dallas lost its first two games. But by the end of the year, Troy and the Cowboys had won enough games to make the play-offs. Troy paid a price during those victories, though. He pulled a hamstring, tore cartilage in his ribs, and separated both shoulders. "It's been a painful year," he said.

In Dallas's first play-off game, against the Green

Bay Packers, Troy threw three touchdown passes and the Cowboys won 27-17. Next, Dallas took on San Francisco to decide which team would go to the Super Bowl. Halfway through the game, Troy was knocked in the head and suffered a concussion. He couldn't even remember his name until early the next day. The Cowboys went on to beat the 49ers anyway, 38-21, and Troy quickly recovered. Next stop, Super Bowl!

The Cowboys would face the Buffalo Bills—the same team they had beaten for the championship one year before. The Bills were eager to avenge their loss, and they played fiercely. At halftime, Buffalo led Dallas by seven points. But in the second half, Troy led his team on one successful drive after another. Dallas won the game 30-13, and the Cowboys were again the world champions.

Following back-to-back Super Bowl victories, Troy came into the 1994 season as one of the premier quarterbacks in the NFL. He broke the club record for consecutive games with a touchdown pass, extending the old record from 12 to 16 games.

In postseason play, Aikman's 94-yard touchdown pass to Alvin Harper was the longest play from scrimmage in NFL postseason history. Despite the Cowboys' 38-28 loss to the San Francisco 49ers, Troy set NFC Championship Game records for attempts, completions, and passing yards.

Troy came on strong again in 1995, but team injuries mounted and a Super Bowl appearance seemed unlikely. Still, Troy led the Cowboys to postseason victories over the Eagles and the Green Bay Packers. Defeating the Packers sent the Cowboys to their third Super Bowl in four years.

Troy started Super Bowl XXX, completing a 47-yard pass to Deion Sanders, then a 19-yard pass to Jay Novacek. Troy didn't play as well after that but allowed no interceptions and came up with 209 passing yards. Just when the game was getting close, Cowboys cornerback Larry Brown made two interceptions off Steelers quarterback Neil O'Donnell.

The Cowboys became the first team ever to win three Super Bowls in four years. Team effort rather than individual achievement was the winning ingredient. Troy later commented, "This is an unselfish team that depends on each other."

Troy wants to play with Dallas for a long time. But now that he is at the top, he has to work hard to make sure he stays there.

"I don't know how I'll handle all this," Troy says of his fame and success, "but it's a nice thing to be worrying about. I've done all right so far."

# College
Passing

| TEAM | YEAR | ATTEMPTS | COMPLETIONS | INTERCEPTIONS | YARDS | % | TDs |
|------|------|----------|-------------|---------------|-------|---|-----|
| Oklahoma | 1984 | 20 | 6 | 3 | 41 | 30.0 | 0 |
| Oklahoma | 1985 | 47 | 27 | 1 | 442 | 57.4 | 1 |
| UCLA | 1987 | 273 | 178 | 8 | 2527 | 65.2 | 17 |
| UCLA | 1988 | 354 | 228 | 9 | 2771 | 64.4 | 24 |

Rushing

| TEAM | YEAR | ATTEMPTS | YARDS | AVERAGE | TDs |
|------|------|----------|-------|---------|-----|
| Oklahoma | 1984 | 12 | 18 | 1.5 | 1 |
| Oklahoma | 1985 | 49 | 93 | 1.9 | 0 |
| UCLA | 1987 | 79 | − 87 | − 1.1 | 2 |
| UCLA | 1988 | 78 | 83 | 1.1 | 1 |

# Dallas Cowboys
Passing—Regular Season

| YEAR | ATTEMPTS | COMPLETIONS | INTERCEPTIONS | YARDS | % | TDs |
|------|----------|-------------|---------------|-------|---|-----|
| 1989 | 293 | 155 | 18 | 1749 | 52.9 | 9 |
| 1990 | 399 | 226 | 18 | 2579 | 56.6 | 11 |
| 1991 | 363 | 237 | 10 | 2754 | 65.3 | 11 |
| 1992 | 473 | 302 | 14 | 3445 | 63.8 | 23 |
| 1993 | 392 | 271 | 6 | 3100 | 69.1 | 15 |
| 1994 | 361 | 233 | 12 | 2676 | 64.5 | 13 |
| 1995 | 432 | 280 | 7 | 3304 | 64.8 | 16 |

Passing—Play-offs

| YEAR | ATTEMPTS | COMPLETIONS | INTERCEPTIONS | YARDS | % | TDs |
|------|----------|-------------|---------------|-------|---|-----|
| 1991 | 16 | 11 | 1 | 114 | 68.8 | 0 |
| 1992 | 89 | 61 | 0 | 795 | 68.5 | 8 |
| 1993 | 82 | 61 | 3 | 686 | 74.4 | 5 |
| 1994 | 83 | 53 | 4 | 717 | 63.9 | 4 |
| 1995 | 80 | 53 | 1 | 717 | 66.3 | 4 |

Rushing—Regular Season

| YEAR | ATTEMPTS | YARDS | AVERAGE | TDs |
|------|----------|-------|---------|-----|
| 1989 | 38 | 302 | 7.9 | 0 |
| 1990 | 40 | 172 | 4.3 | 1 |
| 1991 | 16 | 5 | 0.3 | 1 |
| 1992 | 37 | 105 | 2.8 | 1 |
| 1993 | 32 | 125 | 3.9 | 0 |
| 1994 | 30 | 62 | 2.1 | 1 |
| 1995 | 21 | 32 | 1.5 | 1 |

Rushing—Play-offs

| YEAR | ATTEMPTS | YARDS | AVERAGE | TDs |
|------|----------|-------|---------|-----|
| 1991 | 2 | 0 | 0 | 0 |
| 1992 | 9 | 38 | 4.2 | 0 |
| 1993 | 7 | 28 | 4.0 | 0 |
| 1994 | 2 | 11 | 5.5 | 0 |
| 1995 | 8 | 6 | 1.3 | 0 |

## ACKNOWLEDGMENTS

Photographs used with permission of Herman Brown: pp. 1, 16, 26, 37; Sports-Chrome East/West: pp. 2 (Jeff Carlick), 6 (Louis A. Raynor), 9 (Rob Tringali Jr.), 12 (Mike Corrado), 44-left, 49-left (Rob Tringali Jr.), 49-right (Louis A. Raynor), 57 (Mike Corrado); John Biever: pp. 11, 42, 47, 50; Vernon Biever: p. 14; Al Myatt, Oklahoma Department of Agriculture/Forestry Services: p. 19; Dallas Cowboys Football Club: pp. 21, 32, 41, 44-right; Oklahoma State University: p. 24; UCLA Sports Information Department: p. 29; Brad Harper: pp. 52, 58; Troy Aikman, Texas, Post Office: p. 64.

Front cover: Rob Tringali Jr., SportsChrome East/West
Back cover: Brad Harper